Presented to

Liam

Holy Trinity Church
June 2017

JONAH AND THE WHALE

Jonah

Nineveh

Soldiers

Sailors

Whale

Illustrated by Pamela Johnson

It's fun to Read Along

Here's what you do –

Pictured on this page are some of the people and things featured in this story. Encourage the children to whom you are reading to SEE and SAY the word for each.

Then, as you read the story to them and you come to a picture in place of a word, pause each time for the children to SEE and SAY.

Children love to participate in this kind of storytelling and the SEE and SAY storybooks will become their first choice for reading fun.

ISBN 1-84135-391-4

Copyright © 2000 Award Publications Limited

First published 2000
This edition first published 2005

Published by Award Publications Limited,
1st Floor, 27 Longford Street, London NW1 3DZ

Printed in Malaysia

Waves

King

Sea Captain

Ship

Storm

Vine

People

JONAH AND THE WHALE

Long ago, was sitting in the

 one day when God spoke to

him. God told to go at once to

the great city of and tell the

 and all the there that

their wicked behaviour had offended

God.

Now  didn't want to go and see the and the of . "They are not Hebrews," thought . "Why should I bother with them." So he decided to go far away from . He went down to the sea and paid a to take him to Tarshish on his .

When got on board the

 he was tired, so he lay down

and fell asleep on a coil of .

After a while the sailed away.

A arose, with thunder and lightning. The  were so high that the  and the feared that they would sink. They cried out in fear, "One of us has disobeyed God. That is why this  has struck us." They drew straws to find out who it was. drew the shortest straw.

said to the  , "I am the one who has disobeyed God. If you throw me into the , the  will pass." The did not want to do this but, after they had failed to row to land,  was thrown into the sea. The ceased and the sailed on, as the thanked God.

In the sea,  prayed to God for help. Just as he was about to sink beneath the  , God sent a  , which swallowed him up.

For three days and nights, was inside the , praying all the time, asking God to forgive him for not obeying God and doing as he asked.

Then the spat out on to a beach. "Go to , as I told you before," said God, "and give the there my message."

knew what he had to do, so

he set off again, this time towards the

city of , which was where God

wanted him to go in the first place.

When he arrived at , he said

to all the  and the  in the

city, "In forty days from now,

will be destroyed by God."

When the and the

in heard , they became

afraid of God's anger and were very

sorry for the wrongs they had done.

As a way of showing their regret

for having offended God, all the

 began to go without food and

put on rough clothes made of sacking.

When the told him about

this, the of rose from his

throne, took off his royal robes and

put on clothes made of sacking.

Then the  sat down in ashes

and ordered that not only the

of must go without food and

water, but also all their  .

"Perhaps," said the , "if we show God that we are truly sorry for the wrongs we have done, he will not destroy the city of ."

Meanwhile, was sitting in the outside the city, waiting for  and all its to be destroyed in forty days' time.

When God saw that the  and

all the  and of

were truly sorry, he decided he would

not destroy them.

Now was still sitting in the , sulking because God had not yet destroyed  , ,  ,  and all.

"This is not what I came here for," said to God. "This is why I took a to Tarshish instead of coming here!"

To give some extra shade from the , God caused a to grow beside him. was happy to sit in the shade of this .

The next day God sent a  to

eat the and it withered and

died. was very angry because

he had no shade from the .

God asked , "Are you angry

because the has died?"

 answered, "Yes, God, I am

angry enough to die myself!"

Then God said to 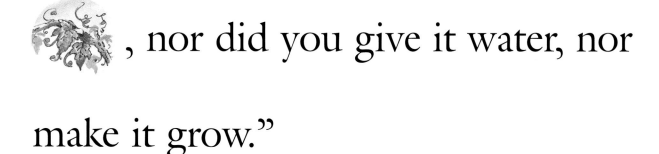 , "You must remember that you did not plant that , nor did you give it water, nor make it grow."

God explained to : "You are

upset by the death of a , which

grew in a night and died in a night.

So why should I not show mercy to

the great city of , which

contains thousands of as well

as many different ?"

Then was ashamed, and

marvelling at God's mercy, he left 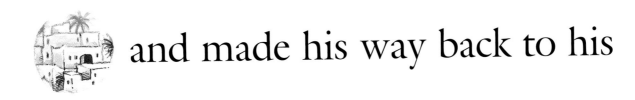 and made his way back to his

own country.